ROME TRAVEL GUIDE 2023

The Most Complete Guide to The Eternal City |
Everything you Need to Know Before Planning Your Trip:
Ancient History, Attractions, Food, Art and Culture

BY

MIKE J. DARCEY

Table of Contents

Introduction

Welcome to Rome, the eternal city! Rome is one of the most visited cities in the world and is known for its rich history, stunning architecture, delicious food, and vibrant culture. In this travel guide, we will provide you with some essential information to help you plan your trip to Rome.

- Shopping: Rome is known for its fashion, and there are many shopping opportunities, from high-end designer stores to small boutiques. The most famous shopping street is Via dei Condotti, but there are also many other shopping districts to explore.
- Nightlife: Rome has a lively nightlife scene with many bars, pubs, and clubs to suit all tastes. The most popular areas for nightlife are Trastevere, Testaccio, and Monti.
- Etiquette: When visiting Rome, it is essential to respect the local culture and customs. Dress modestly when visiting churches and religious sites, and always greet locals with a polite "buongiorno" or "buonasera."

With its rich history, stunning architecture, and delicious cuisine, Rome is a city that should be on every traveler's bucket list. Enjoy your visit!

Chapter 1.
A Brief Historical Overview of Rome

Rome is an ancient city that is the capital of modern Italy. During its early history, Rome was ruled by a succession of kings (most likely Etruscans) that led to the formation of a divided society between the patrician and plebian classes.

Origins

Rome is one of the most important cities in world history. Although the origins of Rome are often attributed to Romulus and Remus, historians agree that the city probably formed earlier. It may have originated as one of the many settlements on the Latium Plain in northern Italy.

During the first century BC, Rome expanded its influence and became one of the most powerful city-states in the world. Roman historians instead relied on their interpretation of religious records and the texts of some laws and treaties to form a chronological framework for the city's history.

While this method provided a relatively accurate representation of events, it was prone to exaggeration and omission. This is especially true of the early history of Rome when there was very little available historical information.

Another problem was that a lot of Rome's historical records were lost or stolen. This made it difficult to document major events in the city's history.

This difficulty in recording historical facts was particularly problematic during the early years of the Roman Republic when there were a lot of conflicts between patricians and plebians. This led to a tumultuous period in which the two groups struggled for power and influence.

Early Rome

Despite this diversity, Rome emerged as an urban society with strong civic institutions and a well-developed legal system. It also remained an important trading hub, drawing on the trade connections to northern and eastern lands. As trade and commerce flourished, a richer culture was developed that linked people and ideas, reflected by the emergence of Roman literature.

As Rome expanded, the population grew rapidly, and the city became a great political and economic center of the ancient world. Under emperors such as Augustus, the empire spread from Britain to Syria and beyond.

While Rome's economy was centered on agriculture, it absorbed a lot of foreign trade. The annexation of Egypt, Sicily, and Tunisia helped increase the supply of grains. This led to an over-reliance on imported slave labor, which eventually put many unemployed Romans out of work.

As the Romans continued to expand their empire, they came under attack from Germanic tribes who invaded parts of Europe. Rather than simply ruling these people as conquered subjects, they began to invite them to become citizens. They were also able to enjoy the benefits of an extensive network of roads that connected all parts of the empire.

Late Roman Empire

It was a vast empire that stretched across the Mediterranean region. In the third century, Rome became weakened by barbarian invasions and religious conflict. This resulted in a decline in the economy and in the morale of the army. As a result, the Roman government had to make serious financial and administrative reforms.

During this time, the Romans fought wars against other nations for territory and power. During the reign of Trajan, the Romans conquered much of Europe, including Dacia and Parthia, and established new cities. While Christians were a minority at first, they eventually became the majority, especially after the rise of Constantine.

However, many of the people who were once Romans began to believe in other religions such as Greek and Jewish beliefs.

The emperors of the fifth and sixth centuries made important reforms that helped to preserve the status of the Empire. These changes included reducing the number of emperors and creating a tetrarchic system that reunited the empire's two halves.

Middle Ages

Rome's location on the Tiber River at a crossroads of several bodies of water made it a very important trade center for a large portion of western Europe. This included the Tyrranhean Sea, Adriatic Sea, Mediterranean Sea, and Ionian Sea. The location also allowed Rome to have easy access to many ancient trade routes that led to other regions of the world.

As the Roman Empire collapsed, a number of Germanic invaders began to raid western European cities and monasteries. This new social and political structure, called feudalism, became the basis of much of Western European life during the Middle Ages. Strong local lords formed an allegiance with their subjects and imposed a strict code of behavior that governed their lives.

In the Middle Ages, a great deal of learning took place and many manuscripts were produced. These texts included religious texts, medical remedies, scientific discoveries, travels to other continents, and prose and verse works.

By the time the 13th century came around, a significant number of manuscripts were being produced in Italy and across Europe. These manuscripts helped to preserve the rich heritage of classical Latin literature and also to generate many new texts that were distinctive to their times.

During the 14th century, a devastating plague known as the Black Plague killed almost half of Europe's population. This pushed the overall life expectancy in Europe down to an average of 45 years, which left many older adults with very little time for productive work.

Renaissance

The Renaissance grew out of a time of great political turmoil and economic change in Italy during the 14th century. The wars of the Spanish, French and German invasions fought over Italy's riches and territories helped to shape this new era in European history.

This period of time also cultivated a new sense of style, based on an idea that artists should paint people and objects in a realistic and naturalistic way, using techniques such as perspective, shadows and light. In some cases, emotion was also infused into their paintings.

A number of religious and dynastic leaders commissioned artists to create portraits, murals, and frescoes that would impress their audience. For example, cities commissioned huge murals for council halls to display civic achievements. And monasteries commissioned artists to paint frescoes in cells and refectories that would inspire their monks to greater devotion.

These artists also sought to translate Greek texts to share knowledge of ancient Greece with the West. Their goal was to make sure that Christians had access to the best of ancient Greek scholarship, which could help them build a solid foundation for their beliefs.

The City's Cultural Heritage

Rome has been one of the most important centers of art and architecture in the world for over 2000 years, with a rich history of artistic and architectural traditions that have influenced the development of Western culture. Here are some of the key features of art and architecture that characterize Rome:

Ancient Roman Art and Architecture: The ancient Romans were renowned for their impressive public buildings, elaborate temples, and monumental sculptures. The architecture of ancient Rome was characterized by the use of arches, vaults, and domes, which allowed for large interior spaces and grand public structures. Examples of ancient Roman architecture that still exist in Rome today include the Colosseum, the Pantheon, and the Roman Forum. Roman art was also known for its realistic portrayals of people and animals, with a focus on achieving accuracy and detail.

Renaissance Art and Architecture: The Renaissance was a period of great artistic and cultural innovation in Rome, with artists and architects exploring new styles and techniques. Renaissance art in Rome was characterized by a renewed interest in classical motifs, including mythological scenes and ancient sculptures. Famous artists of the Renaissance in Rome included Michelangelo, Raphael, and Bernini, who produced some of the city's most iconic works of art, such as the Sistine Chapel ceiling and the Trevi Fountain.

Baroque Art and Architecture: The Baroque period saw a dramatic shift in Rome's artistic and architectural styles, with a focus on grandiose, theatrical designs. Baroque architecture in Rome was characterized by the use of ornate decorations, intricate details, and dynamic curves and angles. Baroque art was also known for its dramatic use of light and shadow, as well as its emotional intensity. Some of the most notable examples of

Baroque art and architecture in Rome include the Church of Sant'Ivo alla Sapienza, the Piazza Navona, and the Fontana dei Quattro Fiumi.

Neoclassical Art and Architecture: In the late 18th and early 19th centuries, Rome became a center for the neoclassical movement, which sought to revive classical forms and motifs in art and architecture. Neoclassical buildings in Rome were characterized by their clean lines, simple shapes, and restrained decoration. Famous examples of neoclassical architecture in Rome include the Palazzo del Quirinale and the Basilica di Santa Maria degli Angeli e dei Martiri.

Modern and Contemporary Art and Architecture: In the 20th century, Rome continued to be a hub of artistic and architectural innovation, with many notable modern and contemporary buildings and works of art. Some of the most famous examples of modern and contemporary architecture in Rome include the MAXXI museum of contemporary art and architecture, designed by Zaha Hadid, and the Auditorium Parco della Musica, designed by Renzo Piano. Rome is also home to a thriving contemporary art scene, with numerous galleries and exhibitions showcasing the work of both established and emerging artists.

Mosaics: Rome is famous for its beautiful mosaics, which have been used to decorate public buildings and churches for centuries. Roman mosaics were made from small pieces of colored glass, stone, or ceramic, and were arranged to create intricate designs and images. Some of the most famous mosaics in Rome include those in the Basilica di San Clemente and the Basilica di Santa Maria in Trastevere.

Fountains: Rome is also known for its many beautiful fountains, which range in style from ancient Roman to Baroque and neoclassical. Fountains were an important feature of public life in Rome, providing clean drinking water and serving as meeting places and social gathering spots. Some of the most famous fountains in Rome include the Trevi Fountain, the Fontana della Barcaccia, and the Fontana dei Quattro Fiumi.

Religious Art: The city is filled with churches and basilicas that are adorned with beautiful frescoes, sculptures, and other works of art. Some of the most famous religious artworks in Rome include Michelangelo's Pieta in St. Peter's Basilica and Caravaggio's Conversion of St. Paul in the Church of Santa Maria del Popolo.

Overall, the art and architecture of Rome are diverse and rich, spanning centuries of cultural history and artistic innovation. From ancient Roman temples and sculptures to modern and contemporary buildings and artworks, Rome continues to inspire.

Chapter 2.
Rome's main attractions

Here is a list of the main attractions in Rome that you absolutely must visit during your trip

- Colosseo (Colosseum): One of the most famous attractions in Rome, the Colosseum is an ancient amphitheater built during the Roman Empire.

- Piazza di Spagna (Spanish Steps): A beautiful public square in the heart of Rome, the Piazza di Spagna is known for its beautiful Baroque architecture and the iconic Spanish Steps, which lead up to the Church of Trinità dei Monti.

- Galleria Borghese (Borghese Gallery): Located in a beautiful villa in the heart of Rome, the Borghese Gallery is home to an impressive collection of art, including works by *Caravaggio, Bernini, and Raphael.*

- Ostia Antica: A well-preserved ancient Roman city located near the coast, Ostia Antica was once a thriving port town.

- Foro Romano (Roman Forum): Once the center of political and social life in ancient Rome, the Roman Forum is now a collection of ruins that give visitors a glimpse into the city's past.

- Città del Vaticano (Vatican City): Example St. Peter's Basilica, the Vatican Museums, and the Sistine Chapel.

- Pantheon: Visitors can explore the temple's interior and admire the artwork and architecture.

- Colosseo e Flora Imperiale (Colosseum and Imperial Forums): A tour that combines visits to the Colosseum and the nearby Imperial Forums, which were once the administrative and commercial center of ancient Rome.

- Musei Capitolini (Capitoline Museums): Located on the Capitoline Hill, the Musei Capitolini house an extensive collection of ancient Roman art and artifacts. Visitors can see sculptures, paintings, and other artworks from the city's history.

- Villa Giulia: A beautiful villa located in the northern part of Rome, Villa Giulia is home to an impressive collection of Etruscan art and artifacts.

- Museo Nazionale Romano (National Roman Museum): A network of four museums located throughout Rome, the National Roman Museum houses an extensive collection of ancient Roman art and artifacts.

- Villa Borghese: A beautiful park located in the heart of Rome, Villa Borghese is home to several museums, gardens, and attractions. Visitors can explore the Galleria Borghese, which houses an impressive collection of art, as well as the Pincio Terrace, which offers stunning views of the city.

- San Pietro in Vincoli (St. Peter in Chains): A beautiful church located near the Colosseum, San Pietro in Vincoli is known for its stunning Michelangelo sculpture, Moses.

Visitors can explore the city's many attractions and museums to learn about its rich cultural heritage and appreciate its beauty.

More attractions

Trastevere

Trastevere is a warren of narrow streets and cloistered piazzas that, for centuries, has served as Rome's working class artisan district. It's a neighborhood that, visually, captures all the best of the Eternal City, and one which has long been a favourite with locals and visitors alike.

Today, it's also one of the trendiest neighborhoods in the city thanks to its diverse nightlife and the many hidden archaeological gems. Trastevere is home to a thriving international community of artists, students and expatriates who love its intricate web of alleys and flower-strewn piazzas.

If you're looking for a quieter slice of Trastevere, check out Santa Cecilia church, which sits in a charming leafy atrium and is filled with stunning mosaics that date from the 1140s. There's also a pretty crypt to explore, as well as an impressive baldachin canopy that soars towards the ceiling.

Villa Borghese

One of Rome's greenlungs, Villa Borghese is home to a number of attractions, including the popular Galleria Borghese. This museum houses a large collection of Italian art and makes a fantastic day trip from the city centre.

The park is also a great place to spend time relaxing after a long walk, having a picnic or simply sitting on the bench and enjoying a book. A tranquil lake and 19th-century style temple are the highlights of this part of the park.

The area is also home to the Bioparco di Roma zoo, which cares for more than 200 animals. Animal lovers should definitely visit this attraction during their stay in Rome!

Catacombs

The Catacombs are underground passageways that were used as burial sites for Jews, pagans and early Christians. They were built next to tuff stone quarrying operations in the outskirts of Rome and the name means "next to the quarry".

St Domitilla is the largest and most extensive of Rome's catacombs. It's 17 kilometers long, on four levels, and was the final resting place of approximately 150,000 people.

Arch of Constantine

The reliefs on the front and sides of the arch are based on spolia from the 2nd century. The roundels above the outer arches feature figures originally from Hadrian's time but have been modified to resemble Constantine.

Trajan's Market

Once considered to be Rome's first "shopping mall", it was commissioned by Emperor Trajan in the late 2nd century and designed by his favorite architect, Apollodorus of Damascus. Thanks to recent excavations, the building is now believed to have served multiple purposes, including as a government office and possibly as a court house.

The complex is made up of six levels connected by a staircase, and consists of scores of shops, known as tabernae. Those on the ground floor faced onto a passageway, while those on the upper floors opened onto a street called Via Biberatica.

Spanish Steps

One of the most well-known sights in Rome, the Spanish Steps are a great place to start your sightseeing. It's also a favorite location for photographers and artists, as the wide stairs provide an inspirational backdrop for their work. This spot is a must-see for those who want to get a sense of the beauty and joy that can be found in Rome.

The steps are also home to a fountain called the Fontana della Barcaccia, or Fountain of the Boat, inspired by a flood that washed a boat all the way from the river up to the square.

St. Peter's

In the basilica's interior, there are many intricate structures and artworks that add to its magnificence. Michelangelo's Pieta, his soaring dome and Bernini's 95ft-high baldachin over the papal altar are just a few of the highlights to look out for.

Besides the main attractions, there are many other chapels, artworks, statues and tombs in and around St. Peter's that are worth visiting as well.

Pantheon

With a dome that has withstood earthquakes and wars for nearly 2,000 years, it's a must-see on any travel itinerary to the Eternal City.

The Pantheon was later transformed into a Christian church and consecrated to Sancta Maria ad Martyres, or Santa Maria of the Martyrs, in 609. It is also home to important tombs, including that of Raphael, the great Italian painter and architect.

Piazza Navona

It's filled with cafes and shops, street performers, artists, and hawkers.

This fountain features a faux ancient Egyptian obelisk and neoclassical sculpture surrounding a glistening basin containing four river gods.

Piazza del Popolo

Piazza del Popolo, located at the foot of the Pincio terrace, is one of Rome's most famous squares.

The square is home to a large ellipse surrounded by an Egyptian obelisk from the Sun Temple of Heliopolis (an obelisk that Augustus brought from Heliopolis to display at the Circus Maximus). It was restored in 1589 under Pope Sixtus V, and erected in this square in 16th-century.

Chapter 3.
The best Restaurants, Clubs and Nightlife

Rome has a diverse and vibrant restaurant scene, offering a range of traditional and contemporary Italian cuisine. Some of the best restaurants in Rome, such as La Pergola and Il Pagliaccio, have earned multiple Michelin stars for their innovative and high-end cuisine.

When it comes to clubs and nightlife, Rome has something for everyone. Like Goa Club, Shari Vari Playhouse, and Akab are just a few examples. Many of these clubs are located in neighborhoods like Testaccio and Trastevere, which are known for their lively nightlife scenes.

For those who prefer a more relaxed evening out, Rome has many charming bars and wine bars in popular areas like Campo de' Fiori and Monti. These areas also offer plenty of opportunities to enjoy aperitivo, a pre-dinner drink and snack that is a popular part of Italian culture.

Restaurants:

La Pergola: This three-Michelin-starred restaurant is located on the top floor of Rome Cavalieri, Waldorf Astoria Hotels & Resorts, and offers panoramic views of the city. It serves innovative Mediterranean cuisine with a focus on seasonal ingredients.

Roscioli: A popular trattoria and deli, Roscioli offers a variety of Roman classics, including pasta alla gricia and cacio e pepe, as well as an extensive wine list.

Pizzeria La Montecarlo: Known for its classic Neapolitan-style pizzas, La Montecarlo offers a casual atmosphere and affordable prices.

Il Pagliaccio: Another three-Michelin-starred restaurant, Il Pagliaccio offers contemporary Italian cuisine with an emphasis on seasonal ingredients.

Clubs:

Goa Club: Located in the Ostiense neighborhood, Goa is a popular club with a focus on electronic music. It has a large dance floor and hosts international DJs.

Shari Vari Playhouse: Housed in a former theater, Shari Vari Playhouse offers a variety of music, from techno to hip hop, and has a lively atmosphere.

Akab: Akab is a popular club in the Testaccio neighborhood with a large dance floor and a mix of music genres.

Room 26: Located near the Vatican, Room 26 is a high-end club with a sleek design and a focus on house and techno music.

Art Cafè: This club, located in the historic center, offers a mix of music genres and a stylish atmosphere.

Nightlife:

Campo de' Fiori: This lively square in the historic center is popular with locals and tourists alike for its bars and restaurants.

Trastevere: This bohemian neighborhood on the west bank of the Tiber River has a lively nightlife scene with a variety of bars and pubs.

Testaccio: Once a working-class neighborhood, Testaccio has become a popular destination for nightlife, with a variety of bars and clubs.

Pigneto: This up-and-coming neighborhood on the east side of Rome has a growing nightlife scene with a variety of bars and restaurants.

Monti: This trendy neighborhood near the Colosseum has a variety of bars and restaurants and is popular with a younger crowd.

The best places to stay

Rome is a city filled with history, culture, and incredible food. Whether you're traveling alone, with your partner, or with your family, there are plenty of great places to stay in Rome. Here are some of the best options:

- Centro Storico: This is the heart of Rome and where you'll find many of the city's most famous landmarks, including the Colosseum, the Pantheon, and the Roman Forum. Staying in the Centro Storico will allow you to experience Rome's history up close, and there are plenty of great hotels and Airbnb rentals in the area.

- Trastevere: It's known for its narrow streets, beautiful piazzas, and lively nightlife. Staying in Trastevere will give you a taste of modern Rome while still being close to many of the city's historic sites.
- Monti: This is a trendy neighborhood located near the Colosseum. It's filled with hip cafes, vintage shops, and art galleries. Monti is a great place to stay if you want to be close to the action but still have a quieter place to retreat to at night.
- Testaccio: This is a working-class neighborhood located south of the city center. It's known for its lively market, incredible street food, and vibrant nightlife. Staying in Testaccio will give you a taste of everyday Roman life and is a great option for budget travelers.
- Vatican City: Staying in Vatican City will allow you to experience the majesty of St. Peter's Basilica, the Vatican Museums, and the Sistine Chapel up close. There are plenty of hotels and Airbnb rentals in the area, and it's a great option for those who want to be close to the Vatican's attractions.
- Piazza Navona: It's located in the Centro Storico and is a great place to stay if you want to be close to many of the city's most famous landmarks.
- Colosseo: Staying in the Colosseo area will allow you to experience the grandeur of ancient Rome up close, and there are plenty of great hotels and Airbnb rentals in the area.
- Aventino: This is a quiet residential neighborhood located on one of Rome's seven hills. Staying in Aventino is a great option for those who want to be close to the city center but still have a peaceful place to retreat to at night.
- Esquilino: This is a multicultural neighborhood located near the Termini train station. It's known for its diverse food scene, colorful markets, and affordable prices. Staying in Esquilino is a great option for budget travelers who want to experience a different side of Rome.
- Campo de' Fiori: This is a lively square located in the Centro Storico, known for its open-air market and bustling nightlife. Staying in Campo de' Fiori will allow you to experience the energy of Rome's nightlife scene up close, and there are plenty of great restaurants and bars in the area.

No matter where you choose to stay in Rome, you'll be surrounded by history, culture, and incredible food. Be sure to take the time to explore the city's many landmarks, museums, and neighborhoods, and don't forget to indulge in some gelato while you're there!

Some recommendations for the best places to stay in Rome based on different budget categories:

Budget accommodations: For those on a tight budget, Rome offers a range of affordable options, including hostels, budget hotels, and Airbnb rentals. Some popular budget areas include the Esquilino and Testaccio neighborhoods, which offer affordable accommodation and are still close to many of the city's attractions.

Mid-range accommodations: For those who want to stay in comfort but still within a moderate budget, Rome offers a range of mid-range hotels and rental apartments. Some popular mid-range areas include Monti and Trastevere, which offer a good mix of comfort and affordability.

Luxury accommodations: Rome has no shortage of high-end luxury hotels, and there are plenty of options for those looking for the ultimate indulgence.

Here are some specific recommendations for each budget category:

Budget accommodations:

The Yellow Hostel: Located in the Esquilino neighborhood, this hostel offers affordable dorms and private rooms.

Hotel Dei Mille: Located in the San Lorenzo neighborhood, this budget hotel offers comfortable rooms at an affordable price.

Airbnb rentals: There are many affordable Airbnb rentals available throughout Rome, particularly in the Testaccio and Trastevere neighborhoods.

Mid-range accommodations:

Domus Sessoriana: Located near the Colosseum, this hotel offers comfortable rooms in a historic building.

Rental in Monti or Trastevere: Many rental apartments are available in these trendy neighborhoods, offering a comfortable and convenient stay.

Luxury accommodations:

Hotel Hassler Roma: Located at the top of the Spanish Steps, this luxury hotel offers panoramic views of Rome and luxurious amenities.

Palazzo Manfredi: Located near the Colosseum, this luxury hotel offers elegant rooms and a Michelin-starred restaurant.

Airbnb rentals in the Centro Storico or Vatican City: Many luxury apartments are available for rent in these areas, offering a luxurious and private stay in the heart of Rome.

Chapter 4.
The Hidden gems

Once a slum and red-light district, Monti is now an under-the-radar hipster enclave filled with tasty restaurants and cool boutiques. It's also a great neighborhood to explore if you want to get off the tourist path and experience local life.

This secret gem is a fascinating way to experience Rome's past. Here, you can see ancient Greek and Roman sculptures alongside giant steam engines!

1. Domus Aurea

Domus Aurea is a must see for anyone visiting Rome, especially as the ruins are still being explored. They haven't yet been fully cleaned up for tourism, so it's best to go on a tour with an expert guide who can explain the history of the site and answer any questions you may have!

As you make your way through the ruins, it's easy to get lost in the beauty of the architecture and enthralled by the artworks. Some of the most striking pieces are those that use anamorphosis and trompe l'oeil techniques to make it look like the rooms have three dimensions.

Another highlight of the palace is the octagonal room with a hole in the ceiling that lets sunlight flood through. This is reminiscent of the Pantheon's oculus and can be really fascinating to watch.

You will also find paintings of Egyptian gods and goddesses inside the palace. These are some of the most interesting paintings of the era and were once very popular amongst Romans.

While most of the frescoes in the palace have been damaged due to water, they are still extremely beautiful. The lighting is good and makes it easy to spot the intricate details and there are some fantastic depictions of Anubis and Hector.

The grottoes in the Domus Aurea were an early inspiration for Renaissance artists, who soon began translating these illustrations into their own works of art. Known as grottesche, these paintings gave rise to a style that was very influential on artists including Raphael and Michelangelo.

2. Galleria Sciarra

If you're a fan of 19th-century art, the Galleria Sciarra is worth a visit. Located just a short walk from the Trevi Fountain, this secluded courtyard stands out as one of Rome's best hidden gems.

It is a beautiful open air courtyard decorated with elaborate frescoes and a vaulted ceiling of iron and glass. The Art Nouveau style is incredibly detailed and enthralling, and the walls of the space are covered in intricate frescoes that celebrate women's virtues.

The courtyard is decorated with a series of stunning frescoes that show the "Glorification of Women." It is the perfect place to soak up some 19th-century Roman culture without having to stray far from your hotel or apartment.

While it isn't the most central of spots, this courtyard is a great way to see some amazing 19th-century art and get a glimpse into the lives of Rome's richer citizens. It's also a great spot to take in some beautiful views of the city.

Another reason why the Galleria Sciarra is such a hidden gem is that it's so accessible. It's only a two-minute walk from the Trevi Fountain, and it's not difficult to find.

As a bonus, it's a quiet, picturesque courtyard with gorgeous views of the Eternal City.

In addition to its secluded location, the Galleria Sciarra is also free to visit. It's not a high priority for tourists, but it's a must-see if you're looking to admire some stunning 19th-century artwork while in the heart of Rome.

If you're looking for some other bucket list-worthy hidden gems in Rome, consider visiting the Aventine Hill. The Aventine also offers an escape from the bustling streets of the Eternal City, making it a great choice for those who want to see more of the capital's history in a single day.

3. Tiber Island

Tiber Island is a hidden gem of Rome that doesn't get enough attention. It's tucked between the historic Trastevere and the Jewish Ghetto, yet it's well worth taking a quick detour from your walking tour of the city center to check out.

The island is one of the most intriguing parts of Rome because it has a long history associated with healing and religion. It's also home to a beautiful Baroque church, San

Bartolomeo all'Isola, and the 16th century hospital Fatebenefratelli, which is still in operation today.

While there are many different legends about the island's origins, the most popular story is that it was formed after the fall of Tarquinius Superbus (510 BC). According to this legend, Romans threw the body of their despised tyrant into the Tiber and dirt and silt accumulated around it, which eventually grew the island.

However, another version of the island's origins is that it was formed when people threw the wheat they had collected in Campo Marzio into the river and it settled on the bottom of the water. Then over time, a variety of other debris was deposited on top of the sediment that made up the island's central core.

It's also worth checking out the Ponte Fabricio, which is the oldest bridge in the city and dates back to 2,000 years. It's a great place to sit and watch the river as you cross over.

If you're looking for a little food, you should try the popular Trattoria Sora Lella. This restaurant has been going strong since 1940 and is a must-try in the city's summer months.

The island is a beautiful spot for a stroll and has several historic bridges. The best-preserved of these is the Ponte Fabricio, which crosses over from the left bank of the Tiber.

Other notable structures on the island include a small obelisk that seems to resemble a mast and an ancient tower called Torre della Pulzella or Tower of the Maid. This medieval tower is positioned at the end of the Ponte Fabricio and features a carving of a young female's head.

4. Museo Nazionale Etrusco di Villa Giulia

Located inside Villa Giulia, one of Rome's most beautiful Renaissance palaces, is the National Etruscan Museum.

This museum is packed with incredible artifacts from the ancient Etruscan civilization. The best part is that it's free to enter!

The museum is incredibly well-curated and you can spend hours exploring the collection. You can find a wide variety of Etruscan artifacts, including a stunning Sarcophagus of the Bridegrooms that's a replica of an actual necropolis found in Cerveteri.

As a bonus, you can take in the gorgeous Villa Giulia gardens as well! You might want to book a guided tour here so that you can take your time to truly appreciate the collection.

In this museum you can find a great assortment of artifacts from the Etruscan necropolis of Banditaccia in Cerveteri, Italy's largest. You can also find some very interesting vases and statues from the Necropolis of Tarquinia.

This is the perfect destination for those who want to learn more about the Etruscans, as they were the earliest of the Romans' neighbors. You'll see everything from a gorgeous stone sarcophagus to beautiful bronze urns.

While this museum is less known compared to other major museums in Rome, it's a very interesting place to visit. It's a great place to learn more about the Etruscans and how they affected Rome and the rest of Europe. There's an entire floor dedicated to these two cultures, which you should definitely check out. This is a small, but very well-curated museum.

Chapter 5.
How to Get in Touch With Local Culture in Rome

Rome is a diverse city with many different cultures.

1. Visit the Pigneto

If you want to feel like a real Roman, you need to get in touch with local culture. This means being willing to adapt to new customs, food, and behaviors that you might not be familiar with. It also means taking the time to learn and speak some Italian while you're in Rome so you can interact with locals and make friends.

One of the best places to do this in Rome is the Pigneto, a neighbourhood that's known for its alternative shops, vintage stores, and diverse bars and restaurants.

This neighborhood is a bit off the beaten path, and its original craft stores and ateliers give it a bohemian flair that makes it the place to go for art-lovers. There's a small, intimate cinema here that shows only independent movies that you'll have to see to believe, and it's a great way to see some unique Italian films.

Another great spot to enjoy some culture is the Anarchic Library, located in Via Braccio da Montone 71/A. It has an extensive collection of books from a variety of cultures, and it's a great place to find an escape from the city for a few hours.

The neighborhood is also home to many clubs and music venues, and there's a great selection of indie bands that perform there. Necci dal 1924 is an iconic watering hole, where locals have been gathering since the late XIX century to drink coffee and chat in the courtyard.

To experience some of the best dining in Rome, try a dining experience at a hand-selected local host's home or private venue. They'll provide you with an amazing meal and make you feel right at home. If you have any dietary restrictions, just ask them ahead of time and they'll do their best to accommodate you.

2. Go to a pub

A pub, or birreria, in Rome is the perfect place to hang out with locals and get the inside scoop on all things Roman. It's also a great way to meet locals who speak English, and who can help you navigate the city's many tourist hotspots.

In the UK, a pub has become a social hub for people to relax and share a drink with friends. In the past, these establishments were typically split into different rooms or bars in order to cater to a wide range of customers. In today's world, such boundaries are unnecessary and a pub is now a great place for anyone to meet new friends.

While you can find a great pub in just about every part of the city, some of the best are located in the more cultural areas. Campo de Fiori is a young, bohemian neighbourhood with a wide range of cafes and restaurants serving delicious aperitivo and coffee.

Another popular area is Trastevere, which is known for its historic alleys and coffe shops. It's a good place to mingle with the local residents, as well as young tourists and students from the universities.

If you are in the mood for a night out, try one of the many bar crawls that combine sightseeing with signature drinks. These are a great way to meet new people and get in touch with local culture, while staying within budget.

The Jerry Thomas Project is an underground bar that's popular among serious drinkers. The secret entrance is hidden behind a staircase, and you'll need to pay a membership fee and find out their daily password.

In addition to being a great spot for a drink, Scholars is also one of the best places to watch all kinds of sporting events. It has over 20 TVs showing everything from American Football to Euro Football championships, Six Nations Rugby, Aussie Rules and even Grand Slam Tennis.

3. Go to a club

When it comes to nightlife, Rome offers a wide range of cool bars, discos and clubs. These night spots are popular among locals, students and tourists alike.

One of the best ways to get in touch with local culture is by attending a club. A club in Rome is a social organization that exists to support members with shared interests and goals. There are service clubs, social activities clubs, political and religious clubs and more.

The main purpose of these clubs is to encourage social interaction and the development of friendships. There are also groups that support specific causes and charities.

For example, the Rome Club, one of the city's biggest clubs, supports the charity organisation CIRCUS MIRA. It also promotes the activities of the charity and organizes various events.

In addition, the club hosts regular parties with live bands and DJs. Moreover, it has a bar and a restaurant.

Located in Testaccio (the most fashionable district), this nightclub is famous for its trendy atmosphere, international music and stylish Romans. Its three rooms offer different music styles, from house and techno to hip hop and alternative.

You'll find a lot of international students and tourists in this club, so make sure to come early. The place is always packed, especially on Fridays.

Another great option is Fanfulla, a unique club combining cinema and music. The club's guests can watch films from a variety of genres and enjoy music from live bands and DJs. The club's atmosphere is also quite unique, as it features a living room style terrace overlooking the Tiber river.

4. Go to a restaurant

Rome is a city with an excellent food culture. You can find many different styles of restaurants from cosy trattorias to Michelin-starred establishments.

Often, the best places to dine in Rome are a little off the tourist trails and away from the main attractions. You may have to make a few trips on the metro or bus, but you will be rewarded with some great meals.

One of the most important things to remember when eating in Rome is that Italians are very serious about their food and take pride in using the freshest local ingredients. You will see this reflected in many of the restaurants you will eat at, but you can also learn how to fully embrace this ethic by taking a cooking class.

Another great option for a more authentic experience is to go on a local tour with one of our hand-selected Roman hosts. These food and wine experts will lead you to the finest spots in town, where you can enjoy a delicious meal and experience the authentic culture of Italy!

Getting in touch with local culture is one of the best ways to enjoy a vacation. By doing so, you can make sure that your trip is unforgettable and that you leave Rome feeling as though you've truly been to the heart of the Eternal City.

5. Go to a museum

If you want to see the best museums in Rome, there are a few tips that can help make your experience easier. Another tip is to visit the museum on the first Sunday of the month, when it is free of charge. You should also take a trip to the MAXXI Museum, which is Rome's newest museum that focuses on modern art. It is designed by Zaha Hadid, the starchitect of the Guggenheim Bilbao in Spain, and showcases work that reflects the current state of art.

It is also worth a visit to the Capitoline Museums, which are a must-see for anyone who wants to get a deeper understanding of the history of this incredible city. There are tours that can be arranged in English, or you can join the general public to enjoy the amazing exhibits.

The Borghese Gallery is one of the top art galleries in Rome and it is definitely worth a visit if you have an interest in Italian art. It is located in the heart of Rome and it has a fantastic collection of sculptures by artists such as Gian Lorenzo Bernini, Titian, Raphael, Caravaggio and Rubens. The Borghese Museum is a great place to see some of the finest art in Rome, but it is important to note that it can be difficult to access. This will ensure that you have a great experience and that you are able to view all the important pieces.

Rome Streets

Alot of this history is visible in the architecture and infrastructure of Rome, a city with a rich history spanning a wide range of centuries. Rome's buildings, monuments, and roads were all constructed in different styles, depending on the era in which they were built. This makes it possible to trace the city's history through its physical structure, from the ancient ruins of the Roman Forum to the Baroque churches and palaces of the 17th century. Among the most famous streets in the world, there are a few that are more iconic than others. There is no better way to get a feel for the real Roman experience than to walk the streets of the city and see what it's like. From the cobblestone streets of the ancient forum to the grand piazzas of the Renaissance, each street of Rome tells its own story. The architecture and infrastructure have evolved over the ages, but still bear the marks of their past, giving the city its unique character. Adding to the grandeur of Rome, its streets are steeped in history, and often bear witness to centuries of artistic, political, and social development. This is why, even today, a stroll through the streets of Rome can be a remarkable journey through time, offering an unparalleled glimpse into the heart of this ancient city.

It is no secret that Rome has a lot of noteworthy streets and landmarks, but some of the most noteworthy ones include Campo de' Fiori - a city square with a market located right in the center of the square, Piazza del Popolo - another historical public square, as well as Via Giulia - a key example of a Renaissance urban planning project. Campo de' Fiori is known for its vibrant atmosphere and lively market, while Piazza del Popolo is a stunning piece of architecture with beautiful fountains, statues, and obelisks. Meanwhile, Via Giulia is an important example of Renaissance architecture, and it boasts several churches and palazzos on either side. It is no surprise then, that this city is a tourist's paradise, offering a variety of historically significant sights that are sure to delight. Yet Rome's allure does not end there; the city's breathtaking array of Roman ruins, including the Colosseum, testify to its rich and lengthy history, and make it an unforgettable experience for all who visit. From the Pantheon to the Spanish Steps, Rome has a wealth of attractions for visitors, both ancient and modern. Its many art galleries, museums and archaeological sites provide insight into the city's past, and its vibrant nightlife, delicious cuisine, and unique architecture make it a truly incomparable destination.

There are many beautiful squares in Rome that are surrounded by striking architecture, such as Piazza dei Mercanti! This square dates back to the Middle Ages and was once the commercial hub of the city. It is surrounded by stunning palazzos and is home to some of the city's most iconic monuments. The square has been beautifully preserved and restored over the centuries and is now one of the most popular spots in the city. It is a magnificent example of a traditional Roman square, with cobblestone streets and a central fountain that is flanked by benches and cafes. Today, it is a vibrant and lively hub of activity, attracting both locals and tourists alike to take in the beauty of the square and the monuments it houses. During the 15th Century, when towns were seeking ways to improve the reliability of trade routes, the term "cobblestone" was first used in England. Streets that are made of cobblestone were actually created by the Romans.

Chapter 6.
Tips to consider when visiting Rome

When planning a visit to Rome, here are some things to consider:

Duration of stay: Rome has many amazing attractions to see, so it's important to consider how long you want to stay.

Attractions to visit: Rome is home to many famous attractions, including the Colosseum, Vatican City, and the Pantheon. Consider purchasing tickets in advance to skip the lines and save time.

Food and dining: Rome is known for its delicious food, so consider trying local specialties like pasta alla carbonara or pizza al taglio. Look for authentic local restaurants and avoid tourist traps.

By considering these factors, you can plan a memorable and enjoyable trip to Rome.

Tips

- Book tickets in advance: Many popular attractions in Rome, such as the Colosseum and Vatican Museums, have long lines, especially during peak season. Purchase tickets in advance to avoid waiting in line. You can also consider booking a tour with skip-the-line access.
- Visit lesser-known attractions: Rome is full of lesser-known attractions that are just as beautiful and interesting as the more popular ones. Consider visiting places like the Appian Way or the Baths of Caracalla, which are usually less crowded.
- Take a walking tour: Walking tours are a great way to explore Rome and learn about the city's history and culture.
- Explore outside of the city center: The city center of Rome is beautiful but can be crowded and touristy. Consider exploring areas outside of the center, such as the Trastevere neighborhood or the Testaccio food market.
- Eat where the locals eat: Avoid restaurants and cafes in touristy areas and instead look for places where locals go to eat. Ask locals for recommendations or do some research online.
- Avoid street vendors and souvenir shops: Street vendors and souvenir shops in popular tourist areas are often overpriced and sell low-quality goods. Look for local markets or boutiques for unique and authentic souvenirs.

By following these tips, you can have a more enjoyable and authentic experience in Rome while avoiding the crowds and tourist traps.

Itinerary Samples

Here are some sample itineraries for organizing your days in Rome based on the length of your trip:

2-3 days:

Day 1: Visit the Colosseum, Roman Forum, and Palatine Hill. In the afternoon, visit the Pantheon and Trevi Fountain.

Day 2: Explore Vatican City, including St. Peter's Basilica and the Vatican Museums. In the afternoon, visit Castel Sant'Angelo and walk along the Tiber River.

Day 3: Take a walking tour of the historic Trastevere neighborhood and explore the Piazza Navona, Campo de' Fiori, and Jewish Ghetto areas.

4-5 days:

Day 1: Visit the Colosseum, Roman Forum, and Palatine Hill. In the afternoon, explore the nearby Monti neighborhood.

Day 2: Explore Vatican City, including St. Peter's Basilica and the Vatican Museums. In the afternoon, visit the Castel Sant'Angelo and the Piazza del Popolo.

Day 3: Take a walking tour of the historic Trastevere neighborhood and explore the Piazza Navona, Campo de' Fiori, and Jewish Ghetto areas.

Day 4: Visit the Borghese Gallery and the nearby Villa Borghese gardens. In the afternoon, explore the Spanish Steps and the Via del Corso shopping district.

Day 5: Take a day trip to the nearby town of Tivoli, which is home to the beautiful Villa d'Este and Villa Adriana.

7+ days:

Day 1-3: Visit the Colosseum, Roman Forum, Palatine Hill, Pantheon, Trevi Fountain, and Monti neighborhood.

Day 4-5: Explore Vatican City, including St. Peter's Basilica and the Vatican Museums. Visit the Castel Sant'Angelo, the Piazza del Popolo, and the Villa Borghese gardens.

Day 6-7: Take a walking tour of the historic Trastevere neighborhood and explore the Piazza Navona, Campo de' Fiori, and Jewish Ghetto areas. Visit the Borghese Gallery and the Spanish Steps.

Day 8-10: Take day trips to nearby towns and attractions such as Tivoli, Ostia Antica, or the Castelli Romani wine region. Alternatively, spend some time relaxing and enjoying the local cuisine.

By organizing your days and prioritizing based on the length of your trip, you can make the most of your time in Rome and experience all the city has to offer.

Best time to visit and save money

Rome is a popular tourist destination that can be visited year-round, but the best time to visit is typically from April to June and from September to November when the weather is mild and crowds are smaller. July and August can be hot and crowded, and many locals go on vacation during these months, so some shops and restaurants may be closed.

To get around Rome safely, it's recommended to use public transportation, such as buses, trams, and the metro, as well as taxis or ride-sharing services. Walking can also be a great way to explore the city, but be aware of pickpockets in crowded areas and keep your valuables secure.

To save time and money in Rome, consider purchasing a Roma Pass or Omnia Card, which provide discounts on attractions and public transportation. Also, try to book tours and tickets in advance to avoid waiting in long lines at popular sites like the Colosseum and Vatican City. Finally, consider staying in a hotel or Airbnb outside of the city center, where prices tend to be lower, and try to dine at local trattorias and pizzerias instead of more touristy restaurants.

Additionally, here are some more tips to save time and money while visiting Rome:

Plan ahead: This can help you avoid wasting time figuring out where to go next and allow you to see more in a shorter amount of time.

Use free resources: Rome is home to many historic sites and monuments that are free to visit, such as the Pantheon and Trevi Fountain. Check out free walking tours or audio guides to learn more about the city's history and culture.

Eat like a local: Rome is known for its delicious cuisine, but eating at touristy restaurants can be expensive. Look for local trattorias and pizzerias to try traditional dishes like carbonara and margherita pizza at more affordable prices.

Take advantage of happy hour: Many bars and restaurants offer "aperitivo" or happy hour specials where you can get a drink and small bites for a discounted price. This can be a great way to try new foods and drinks while saving money.

Consider a bike rental: Renting a bike can be a fun and affordable way to explore Rome's historic neighborhoods and parks. Look for bike rental shops near major tourist sites and plan your route in advance.

Chapter 7.
Basics on the Language in Rome

Italian is a Romance language, and it shares a lot of vocabulary with other Romance languages such as Spanish, Portuguese, and French. However, it also has some unique vocabulary that you'll need to learn if you want to communicate effectively with locals in Italy. Here are some essential Italian phrases and words you should know:

Ciao - This is a casual way of saying "hello" or "goodbye". It's appropriate for use with friends or acquaintances.

Buongiorno - This means "good morning" and is a polite way to greet someone during the day.

Buonasera - This means "good evening" and is a polite way to greet someone in the evening.

Grazie - This means "thank you", and it's important to use it whenever someone does something for you or helps you in any way.

Prego - This is a versatile word that can mean "you're welcome", or "go ahead", depending on the context.

Parla inglese? - This means "do you speak English?" It's a useful phrase to know if you're having trouble communicating in Italian.

Per favore - This means "please" and is another polite way to make a request or ask for something.

Scusi, dove si trova...? - This means "excuse me, where is...?" You can use it when you need to ask for directions.

Posso avere...? - This means "can I have...?" It's a useful phrase to know when you're ordering food or drinks.

Vorrei... - This means "I would like..." and is another useful phrase to use when ordering in a restaurant or café.

Quanto costa? - This means "how much does it cost?" It's an important phrase to know when shopping or using public transportation.

Che ora è? - This means "what time is it?" You can use it to ask for the time of day.

Mi chiamo... - This means "my name is..." and is a way to introduce yourself to others.

Non capisco - This means "I don't understand" and can be useful if someone is speaking too fast or using unfamiliar vocabulary.

These are just a few of the many Italian phrases and words you'll need to know if you want to communicate effectively with locals in Italy. It's important to practice speaking and listening in Italian as much as possible to become comfortable with the language and to improve your ability to communicate.

Things to Do For Free or With Limited Budget in Rome

While you can easily spend a lot of money exploring the Eternal City, it's not always necessary. There are plenty of great places to go in Rome that are totally free or cheaply priced!

One of my favourite places to visit in Rome is Villa Borghese. It's a large park with a zoo located within it that's perfect for kids.

1. Visit Villa Borghese

If you want to go a step further, you can visit Villa Borghese – an expansive green area located within the heart of the city. This pond-lined area is ideal for families with kids and is a great place to relax.

If you're looking for something to do that will help you develop your child's appreciation for art, there are plenty of things to do at the Galleria Nazionale d'Arte Moderna (GNAM). They run creative workshops alongside exhibitions that will help your little ones explore and appreciate art in an environment that's fun for them.

2. Take a Tour of the Colosseum

One of the world's greatest wonders, the Colosseum is an iconic site and a must-see while in Rome. There are many ways to get there, including public transportation, taxi, and Uber.

To avoid the crowds, consider taking a tour with an expert local guide who will show you around the structure and help you to understand it better. These tours often come with special access to non-public areas of the Colosseum, which you won't be able to visit on your own.

The underground chambers and top tiers of the arena are also available on certain tours, so you'll have a chance to see this area, which is normally off-limits for regular visitors.

If you want to skip the lines and explore the Colosseum with an expert, try a tour that visits both the Colosseum and Roman Forum, which is usually combined into a single ticket. Alternatively, you could also consider a self-guided tour to the Colosseum, as this is one of the best ways to see the monument.

3. Explore the Roman Forum

It was also home to many of the city's most iconic buildings and monuments. As with many historical sites, it's best to explore the Roman Forum with a guide.

Once you've finished exploring the Forum, you can easily reach other areas of Rome by foot or public transport. It's a great way to save time and money while you explore the city.

4. Take a Tour of the Vatican

The Vatican Museums contain an extensive collection of works spanning from classical antiquities to modern religious art. Among the best are Raphael's Rooms and Niccoline Chapel, as well as the New Wing and Pio Clementino Museum.

A guided tour is recommended when visiting the Vatican, especially if you're not sure what to expect or how to navigate it all.

The easiest way to reach the Vatican is by public transport. You can use the 40 or 64 buses to get from Roma Termini (the city's main train station) to just outside the Vatican. You can then walk from there.

5. Visit a Museum

Rome is a city that is rich in history, and kids will love to learn more about the places they visit. Many of the city's landmarks are free to visit, and this is one way that you can encourage kids to explore the area without having to spend much money.

The Colosseum is a top place for families to visit, as it's both a fun and educational experience for children. You can also visit the Roman Forum and Palatine Hill, which are great places for kids to learn more about the history of the city.

For even more art, you can visit the Castel Sant'Angelo. Parts of this ancient castle date back nearly 1,900 years, and it's still an impressive structure. For a great day out with the family, take a walk around the grounds and enjoy the views of the city from the lookout point at the top.

6. Visit a Fountain

While you can't avoid the traffic and chaos that fills Rome, there are still plenty of things you can do with your kids that won't cost a fortune. The best one is definitely a visit to the famous fountain in Piazza di Trevi, a rococo-style beauty that is sure to leave you speechless.

The fountain's water is sourced from ancient Roman aqueducts, so it's filled with the freshest water in the city. It's also a great place to capture a romantic picture, but you'll want to avoid visiting during peak times of the day or late at night because it can be overwhelming.

If you're looking for a family-friendly art gallery in Rome, check out GNAM (Galleria Nazionale d'Arte Moderna). They run regular tours and workshops to cultivate appreciation of contemporary art in kids.

Another free thing to do in Rome is to walk the famous Spanish Steps. You'll be rewarded with stunning views of the city from the top. Make sure you climb the stairs before they're closed and take a look at the nearby Chiesa della Trinita dei Monti, which is free to enter.

7. Take a Restaurant Tour

Rome is an incredible city to explore, with everything from magnificent historic buildings and monuments to quiet parks and quaint squares. The city is a great place to take kids as they can explore the landmarks and learn about the culture without having to worry about getting lost or being rushed!

Another great way to see the city and get a taste of its amazing food is by taking a restaurant tour. These tours take you to local restaurants in each neighborhood and allow you to try out the most popular cuisine.

For example, the Jewish Ghetto tour takes you through Rome's historic ghetto and lets you sample some of the region's famous foods like fried artichokes and cheesy suppli. You'll also stop at a local wine bar where you can enjoy delicious Italian prosciutto and a cheese board.

Both of these tours also include a short walking tour of the city's main sights, piazzas, and hidden gems so you can make the most out of your time in Rome! It's also a great way to find some places you'll want to visit later on in your trip.

8. Visit a Zoo

If your kids are animal lovers, the Bioparco di Roma zoological garden is a great place to spend a day with them. Here they can see a wide range of large and small animals from all over the world.

The park is a short walk from the Borghese Palace or it's easy to get on tram line 3 and 19. It's free of charge and there are plenty of places to picnic, relax on the grass or hire bikes.

It's also a great way to take a break from the hustle and bustle of city life. If you want a more active experience, you can join one of the zoo's daily feeding sessions or book onto a guided tour to learn more about their habitats and conservation efforts.

If you want to take a trip to the zoo without spending too much money, it's worth buying a skip-the-line ticket. This will allow you to skip the long queues and have more time exploring the zoo with your children.

Best Market for food, souvenirs

Rome is a city that offers a wealth of shopping options, including food markets, souvenir shops, art galleries, and fashion boutiques. Here are some of the best markets in Rome for food, souvenirs, art, and fashion:

Mercato di Testaccio - Best Market for Food

Located in the Testaccio neighborhood, this market is considered one of Rome's best food markets. It offers a wide variety of fresh produce, meats, seafood, and baked goods, as well as a selection of gourmet food products from all over Italy. Visitors can also sample local specialties, including pizza bianca and porchetta, at the market's street food stalls.

Campo de' Fiori Market - Best Market for Souvenirs

Located in the heart of Rome, Campo de' Fiori is one of the city's oldest and most popular markets. It offers a wide range of souvenirs, including handcrafted leather goods, jewelry, and pottery. Visitors can also purchase local food products, including cheeses, meats, and wine, as well as fresh flowers and produce.

Mercato Monti - Best Market for Art and Fashion

Mercato Monti is a trendy indoor market that features a rotating selection of vendors selling art, vintage clothing, and handmade accessories. Visitors can also enjoy live music and street food while browsing the market's stalls.

Piazza del Popolo Market - Best Market for Antique Shopping

Visitors can also find a selection of books, coins, and other collectibles. The market is a great place to browse for unique and one-of-a-kind souvenirs.

Mercato Centrale - Best Market for Gourmet Food

Located in the historic Termini Station, Mercato Centrale is a food hall that features a variety of gourmet food vendors. Visitors can sample a wide range of Italian specialties, including pizza, pasta, and gelato, as well as a selection of wines and craft beers.

Whether you're in search of fresh produce, unique souvenirs, or trendy fashion items, Rome's markets offer something for everyone. Be sure to visit these markets to experience the city's vibrant shopping scene and discover some of its best culinary offerings.

Best Budget

The city of Rome has often been considered famous for having an overpriced reputation. This is due to factors such as the high cost of living, tourism, and the limited supply of goods and services. Additionally, the city's popularity as a tourist destination led to many businesses raising their prices to capitalize on the influx of visitors. If you are able to book your hotels in advance and make a reasonable amount of preparation, then you can travel within Rome for under €50 - €60 per day with a reasonable amount of planning. During the months of November to March, you might find it easier to plan your trip to Rome. This is because during the colder months, the prices of accommodation tend to drop, as there are fewer tourists. Additionally, during the weekdays, prices tend to be lower than during the weekends, so it is more convenient to schedule your trip for Monday to Thursday if possible. Planning a trip to Rome during these colder months is similar to buying a winter coat at the end of the season when prices are drastically reduced. It is a much smarter decision to buy during the off-season when you can get a better deal.

As a result of this low season, accommodation and transportation prices significantly reduce compared to the rest of the year. This is because fewer people are travelling during the colder months and businesses are trying to promote their services in order to attract customers. Therefore, they are offering discounts and cheaper rates to incentivize people to travel to Rome. Purchase your tickets online for all the attractions and monuments that you want to visit, so that you do not have to wait in line to buy them. There will be a number of discounts that you should be able to take advantage of. If you are intending to eat at a restaurant for a meal, try taking a seat at the bar whenever you are there. Airfare and lodging costs are often lower during this time of year as well, so you can save money on your travel expenses. Furthermore, many attractions offer discounted ticket prices and other discounts during this time of year. Additionally, restaurants often charge less for meals if you sit at the bar rather than at a table.

As a matter of fact, in Italian restaurants, it is not uncommon for the table price to be changed from time to time. The Italian restaurant business is highly competitive and it is not uncommon for restaurant owners to adjust table prices to stay competitive. Additionally, the cost of ingredients or labor can also cause table prices to change from time to time. As such, Italian restaurants often have to stay nimble and adjust their table prices accordingly to stay competitive and ensure they are providing the highest value for their customers. Get yourself a Roman Pass and see what the city has to offer. Using this pass, you will be able to visit up to two landmarks in the city for free. You will also be able to take advantage of discounted entrance to other major attractions, as well as unlimited free use of the public transport system in the city. The most enjoyable way to enjoy your stay in Rome is to ditch public transport and travel around by foot to make the most of it! Located in the center of the city, there are quite a number of monuments and attractions to see. This pass allows you to save money while exploring the city, as you can visit two landmarks for free and get discounted entrance to other attractions. Additionally, traveling by foot provides a unique experience that you wouldn't get from public transport, as you can take in the sights and sounds of the city at your own pace. Take advantage of this opportunity to truly appreciate the city, as it offers a unique perspective of the monuments, attractions, and sounds that make the city so vibrant.

Chapter 8.
The Rome's typical wines, foods and traditions

It's not uncommon to find local, artisan wine makers making some of the country's best offerings. This is a good thing since the quality has risen dramatically in recent years thanks to the fertile soils, regular sea breezes and an old-fashioned cooperative culture.

Wines

Bellone

One of the best-known wine grapes in Rome is Bellone, a variety that has been around since Roman times. It traces its ancient origins in the Castelli Romani area, and is still cultivated there. It can also be found in the coastal areas of Anzio and Nettuno, but it's rarely found elsewhere outside Lazio.

Bellone's olfactory range is very fresh with fruity notes of grapefruit and peach, nuanced by honey and almond funds. It is full-bodied and elegant, with a pleasant acidity that is suitable for aging in the bottle.

It's also easy to drink and is well-suited for young palates. It pairs well with a wide range of dishes, particularly those that have a strong presence of herbs or vegetables.

In fact, it's traditionally served with soups containing broad beans and herb-flavoured risottos. It's also a good companion to unseasoned pecorino Romano.

For those who love wines from the region of Lazio, Bellone is a must. It's a fascinating grape that can stand on its own and is often included in blends from other regions.

At the recent Vinitaly, we tasted a few different Bellones including one from Casale del Giglio, a winery that has worked for years to reintroduce native Lazio varieties into the area. They're now producing Anthium, a 100% Bellone, which is proving to be an exciting and interesting white wine from this region.

They've made it with their 30-year old vines that went through a 3-month maturation on fine lees, and malolactic fermentation. In the end, the result is a complex and harmonious wine, with strong notes of the volcanic soil where it's grown and a ripe and rich fruit that's perfect for long aging in the bottle.

It's a pale yellow with beautiful golden hues, with a lovely olfactory range of citrus and light mineral accents. It's full-bodied and elegant, with a persistent aftertaste. It's an excellent choice for a lunch or dinner and is ideal with fried fish.

Cesanese

Rome's typical wines, which were praised in ancient literature and a lot of history, have always been made using grapes that grow locally around the city. Among these, the most famous ones are Abbuoto, a grape used to make Caecubum - the wine that Pliny the Elder and Horace praises - and Malvasia, which makes the famous Frascati white.

Cesanese is one of the most important native grapes of Lazio. It thrives on hillsides, arid coastal areas and even in warm locations around Rome itself. The grape is a complex one, with a unique aromatic nature and velvety elegance that can be appreciated in all its glory in the finest quality versions.

Its ancestry has been traced back to at least 2000 years ago, making it the oldest of the terroir-specific Italian wines. It grows in the Castelli Romani region and is famous for producing a soft and rich white wine that has always been in symbiosis with the city's cuisine, 'cucina romana'.

There are three appellations for the grape, including two DOCs and one DOCG (denominazione di origine controllata). The first is Cesanese del Piglio, which covers the winemaking area of Piglio. The other two are Cesanese di Olevano Romano and Cesanese di Affile.

All of these grapes, which are all grown on hill slopes, require careful cultivation to ensure the grapes develop a full range of flavors. The climate of the vineyard and the terroir are particularly important to these wines.

Both the grape and the winemaking region are a defining part of Lazio's identity. Like its fellow indigenous grapes, nebbiolo and nerello mascalese, cesanese is hypersensitive to its terroir and requires a particular degree of heat for ripening.

The ripening period is quite long, with some Cesanese taking up to two years to reach its peak. The wines are characterized by floral and spicy notes along with an inherent bitterness, which can be very pleasant or unpleasant.

It is also possible to make sweet red still wines and sparkling wines from this grape. These are often made at the time of harvest to give them a sweet taste and have fruity strawberry notes.

Frascati

The Romans are a wine-loving people and they have been guzzling Frascati wines in their pasta lunches for centuries. Despite being overshadowed by Chianti, Frascati is one of the region's most popular wines, especially among tourists.

The viticultural area of Frascati extends beyond the town to the nearby Colli Albani hilltops. These volcanic soils produce grapes with a high concentration of potassium and acidity, both of which are essential for growing and fermenting grapes.

In the 1980s, Frascati was a top selling Italian wine and, for many years, it was one of Italy's best selling wines worldwide. However, in the 1990s it began to lose its popularity as quality suffered and production was pushed to the lower end of the market.

Today, however, there is a new generation of Frascati producers who are reviving the brand and producing a wine that deserves to be on everyone's list when visiting Rome. They are also working to promote the DOC in order to protect the region from development and ensure that the grapes are always produced in a quality manner.

Dry table wines are the most popular, labelled Novello, Superiore or Novello Superiore, and they are made from at least 50% Malvasia Bianca di Candia (Malvasia Puntinata in Lazio) grapes. They may be paired with other grapes, such as Trebbiano Toscano or Greco Bianco, that add floral notes and acidity to the blend.

These are great with light pasta dishes and vegetables as they have a refreshing and crisp taste, which works well when the food is hot and spicy. The low alcohol content makes it a perfect wine for summer evenings.

They are also a good pairing with Antipasto, which is an assortment of bite-sized snacks such as marinated vegetables, pickled foods and cured meats that are meant to whet your appetite before you sit down and dine. The acidity in the wine helps wash away all the salt and fat in these foods, allowing you to enjoy them even more.

They can be paired with a variety of foods, but are most commonly enjoyed with fresh fish and other seafood. The citrus and floral notes in Frascati pair perfectly with a wide range of other foods as well.

Lazio

Rome is famous for its cuisine, but you can also find some really delicious wines. The Lazio region around Rome has its own wine heritage that dates back to Etruscan times. The most popular grapes are Malvasia and Trebbiano, but the region is also known for the Cesanese.

There are three DOCs producing this rich, red wine. They are: Cesanese di Genazzano, Cesanese Comune and Cesanese d'Affile. These wines are all fruity and well-structured.

They are made from a blend of Sangiovese, Merlot, Montepulciano and Ciliegiolo. The wine is aged for at least two years and is medium-bodied with flavors of dark cherry, raspberries, blueberries and a hint of vanilla.

It is a great match with rich sauces and fatty dried sausages, or with some of the many pasta dishes found in Lazio (I particularly like a classic Cacio e Pepe). If you are looking for something more sparkly, look out for Raffaele Schiavella's Blanc de Noir sparkling white wine, which is made from the cesanese grape using the metodo classico, or champagne method.

Another of the lesser-known white grapes growing in Lazio is Bellone, which is largely grown in the Castelli Romani hills just southeast of Rome. It has a more structured, fragrant aroma and is often blended with Malvasia or Grechetto.

These wines are very pleasant to drink and pair with most foods you'll find in the region. They are not the most expensive, but they are a great value for their quality and are worth considering.

The winery in the town of Frascati, just 20 miles from Rome, makes one of the most popular wines in Lazio. They produce both dry and sweet whites, including a cannellino (sweet) wine.

If you are in the area, take the time to explore the vineyards. This is the best way to get a taste of the local grapes and enjoy the beautiful countryside.

You can also take a trip to Lake Bracciano or the Aurunci Mountains, which are both worth visiting.

Foods and Traditions

Rome is famous for its delicious and hearty cuisine, which has its roots in ancient Roman and Italian traditions. Here are some typical foods and traditions you can expect to experience in Rome:

- Pasta dishes - Rome is known for its pasta dishes, particularly the classic carbonara made with eggs, cheese, guanciale (cured pork cheek), and black pepper. Another popular dish is cacio e pepe, a simple but delicious pasta dish made with pecorino cheese and black pepper.
- Pizza al taglio - Rome's version of pizza is baked on a thin, crispy crust and served by the slice. It's a popular street food and can be found at many local pizzerias.

- Supplì - This is a popular Roman street food, similar to arancini, that consists of deep-fried balls of rice filled with mozzarella cheese and ragù (meat sauce).
- Roman artichokes - A specialty of the Roman cuisine, carciofi alla romana is a dish made with artichokes cooked with olive oil, garlic, and mint, and then braised in a savory broth until tender.
- Gelato - Rome has a long tradition of making artisanal gelato, and you'll find many gelaterias offering a variety of flavors made with fresh, seasonal ingredients.
- Aperitivo - This is a traditional pre-dinner drink and snack that's popular in Rome. It typically involves sipping a refreshing cocktail while enjoying some light appetizers, such as olives, cheese, and cured meats.
- Festa della Befana - This is a traditional Italian holiday that takes place on January 6th, when a witch named La Befana is said to fly on her broomstick to deliver gifts to children who have been good. It's a fun and festive celebration that includes parades, music, and food.
- Pasqua - Easter is a big holiday in Rome, and it's celebrated with traditional foods such as lamb, artichokes, and sweet Easter bread.
- Ferragosto - This is a popular summer holiday in Rome, where many locals take the opportunity to escape the city and head to the coast or the mountains for a day trip or a longer vacation.

Rome's cuisine and traditions are deeply rooted in the city's history and culture, and they offer a delicious and unique way to experience the city's rich heritage. Whether you're enjoying a classic pasta dish, sampling street food, or sipping an aperitivo, you'll find that Rome's food and traditions are an integral part of its charm and allure.

Transport

Transportation in Rome is extensive and includes buses, trams, metro lines, taxis, and other forms of public transportation. Buses and cabs are among the most commonly used means of transportation in Rome.

Buses in Rome:

The buses in Rome are operated by ATAC, the local public transport company. The buses operate from 5:30 am to midnight, with some night buses running until 5:00 am. The bus system is quite extensive, covering the city and its outskirts. The bus routes are numbered and identified by the final destination.

To use the bus in Rome, you need to purchase a ticket before boarding. You can buy tickets at tobacco shops, newsstands, and ticket vending machines located at major bus stops. The ticket cost is the same for all public transportation means, including buses and metro lines. It costs €1.50 per ticket and is valid for 100 minutes from the first validation. You can also buy a day ticket that costs €7.00 and is valid for unlimited rides until midnight of the same day.

Cabs in Rome:

The official taxi companies in Rome are white, and their cars have a distinctive "TAXI" sign on the roof. You should avoid using unauthorized taxi drivers, known as "pirate" taxis, as they charge significantly higher rates than official taxis.

The cost of a taxi ride in Rome is determined by a meter, and fares are based on the distance traveled and the time spent in traffic. There is a minimum charge of €3.00, and rates are higher at night, on weekends, and during public holidays.

In summary, transportation in Rome is extensive and offers several options, including buses and cabs. Buses are operated by ATAC, and tickets can be purchased before boarding. Cabs are readily available, and fares are determined by a meter.

In addition to buses and cabs, Rome also has a metro system with three lines: A (orange), B (blue), and C (green). The metro operates from 5:30 am to 11:30 pm, with extended hours on weekends and public holidays. However, you need to remember to validate your ticket before entering the station and keep it with you for the duration of your journey.

Another option for transportation in Rome is the tram system. The trams are operated by ATAC, and they cover some areas that are not served by the metro. The trams operate from 5:30 am to midnight, with some night trams running until 2:30 am

While buses and cabs are the most commonly used means of transportation, the metro and tram systems are also convenient options. Regardless of the mode of transportation you choose, it's important to purchase a ticket before boarding and remember to validate it. Additionally, be sure to use official taxis to avoid being overcharged.

Packing Tips

If you're planning a trip to Rome, it's important to pack appropriately for the city's climate and cultural customs.

Insect repellent: During the summer months, mosquitoes and other insects can be quite prevalent in Rome. Be sure to pack insect repellent to keep them at bay.

Power adapter: Italy uses a different electrical outlet and voltage than many other countries, so be sure to bring a power adapter to charge your electronics.

Cash and credit cards: Rome is a cash-based society, so it's a good idea to carry some euros with you. However, most places also accept credit cards.

Guidebook and maps: While you can certainly explore Rome on your own, a guidebook and maps can be helpful in navigating the city's many attractions.

Camera: Rome is a beautiful city with many picturesque sights, so be sure to bring a camera to capture your memories.

Medications and first-aid kit: If you take any prescription medications, be sure to bring enough for the duration of your trip. It's also a good idea to pack a small first-aid kit with basic supplies like bandages, pain relievers, and antiseptic.

Respectful attire: Rome is a city with a rich cultural history, and it's important to respect its traditions and customs.

Things to Carry When Visiting Rome

When you're packing for a trip to Rome, you want to make sure that you have all the essentials. From the clothes that you wear to the shoes that you wear, there are some things that you should always carry on your trip.

It's a must-have if you're planning on visiting the city during the winter or summer and it's a great way to protect yourself from rain.

Passport

If you're traveling internationally, be sure to bring your passport and any necessary visas or travel documents.

Plane tickets

Be sure to bring your plane tickets and any other travel documents, such as confirmation emails or hotel reservations.

Credit cards and cash

Bring at least one credit card and some cash to use for expenses during your trip.

Travel insurance

Consider purchasing travel insurance to protect against unexpected events, such as trip cancellations or medical emergencies.

Travel adapter

Rome uses the same electrical outlets as the rest of Europe, and you may need a universal adapter to charge your devices.

Headphones

Pack a pair of headphones to use on the plane or when you need some quiet time.

Camera and charger

Bring a camera and a charger to capture memories of your trip.

Toiletries

Pack a small bag with essential toiletries, including toothpaste, toothbrush, shampoo, and soap.

Sunglasses

Pack a pair of sunglasses to protect your eyes from the sun's rays.

Sunscreen

Pack sunscreen with a high SPF to protect your skin from the sun's harmful rays.

Hat

A hat can be helpful for protecting your face and eyes from the sun's rays.

Light raincoat

Rome can be rainy at times, and it can be helpful to pack a light raincoat or umbrella in case of inclement weather.

Comfortable shoes

Rome is a city that is best explored on foot, and you will likely do a lot of walking while you're in the city.

Travel documents

In addition to your passport and plane tickets, consider bringing any other necessary travel documents, such as travel visas or vaccination records.

Travel insurance documents

If you've purchased travel insurance, be sure to bring your policy documents with you in case you need to file a claim.

Travel itinerary

Consider packing a copy of your travel itinerary, including your flight and hotel information, to help you stay organized during your trip.

Maps and guidebooks

Pack a map or guidebook to help you navigate the city and find your way around Rome.

Water bottle

Pack a refillable water bottle and fill it up at public fountains or at your accommodation to stay hydrated while you're in the city.

Snacks

Pack some non-perishable snacks, such as granola bars or nuts, to help keep you fueled during your trip.

Lightweight and versatile clothes

Pack lightweight and versatile clothes that can be mixed and matched to create different outfits.

Layers

Rome's weather can be unpredictable, and it can be helpful to pack layers so that you can adjust to the temperature.

Swimsuit

If you plan to spend time at the beach or at a pool, be sure to pack a swimsuit and beach towels.

Umbrella

Pack a compact umbrella to use in case of inclement weather.

Small backpack or cross-body bag

Pack a small backpack or cross-body bag to keep your valuables close and secure while you're out and about in Rome.

Personal identification

Bring some form of identification, such as a driver's license or ID card, in case you need to prove your identity.

Travel-size laundry detergent

If you're staying in a self-catering accommodation or plan to do some laundry while you're in Rome, consider packing some travel-size laundry detergent.

Travel-size laundry bag

A travel-size laundry bag can be helpful for organizing your dirty laundry while you're on the road.

Passport holder

Pack a passport holder to keep your passport and other important documents safe and organized.

Shirts

If you are visiting Rome during the summer, it's important to pack a few light cotton shirts and a pair of linen pants or jeans. This will keep you comfortable in the hot weather and will allow you to comfortably visit museums and churches without worrying about overheating.

Shirts should be light in color and have a loose fit, so that you can easily button them up when you need to. You should also avoid t-shirts that have too much detail or structure. Instead, opt for crisp, well-kept shirts that will not stick out in a crowd and will look neat and clean no matter where you are.

You will be walking a lot in Rome, so you should make sure to bring good shoes. Fashion sneakers (summer, breathable models) are the best option, and you should also consider a good pair of sandals that are comfortable for tackling uneven cobblestone streets.

One of the things that you can expect from Italians is that they love wearing bright and vibrant colors. This is especially true in Rome since they have about three times more sunlight than the northern half of Europe, so it's a great idea to pack clothing that has an element of sunshine in it.

In addition to this, you should also consider bringing a scarf. Scarves are extremely popular in Rome, and you'll likely see many people wear them both during the day and evenings.

Finally, men should also pack a pair of suspenders. These are a great accessory to have on hand, and they go with most styles of tops and t-shirts.

Suspenders are a great way to dress up your t-shirt and add some character to your outfit, so be sure to include them in your suitcase! They are also a great way to show off your unique style, so don't miss out on this accessory when packing for Rome.

This is because of the size and age of these buildings. To be respectful of the locals, avoid short skirts, strappy tops and anything that leaves your back or stomach exposed.

Shoes

If you're going to be in Rome for a while, you'll need to bring a few things to make the trip more comfortable and enjoyable. One of the most important items you'll want to pack is a pair of shoes. While flip flops may be easy to wear and keep your feet cool in the summer, they won't provide enough support when you're exploring the cobblestone streets of Rome.

The key to choosing good shoes is to find ones that look great and are also comfortable to wear. We suggest opting for a pair of stylish walking boots like Teva Chelsea boots, Blondo Waterproof ankle boot, or Camper ankle boots.

These walking shoes are also great for protecting your feet when walking on uneven surfaces like Rome's cobblestone streets. While they're not the best option for fashion-focused travelers, they're a good choice if you're looking for a comfortable and stylish alternative to sandals or sneakers that can be worn with both dresses and pants.

Another item that's worth packing is a scarf or cardigan. These can be handy for keeping your shoulders and neck covered while visiting churches or other religious buildings, and they're also a stylish accessory that you can throw on over your clothes for when the weather turns colder in spring or fall.

Lastly, you'll want to have a raincoat or a lightweight jacket with you at all times. You'll be walking a lot in Rome and the sun can be very hot during the summer, so it's important to have a cover-up that can protect you from the elements while you explore the city.

For men, a classic pair of dark jeans is a great choice when visiting Rome in the summer. For women, a light-weight dress or skirt is also a good idea when visiting in the summer.

While you may not be able to choose what you wear in Rome, it's important to remember that Italians are sharp dressers. They'll notice if you're wearing short skirts or booty shorts, so it's best to go for a more conservative outfit.

Bag

When it comes to packing for your trip to Rome, you'll want to pack items that are both stylish and comfortable. Whether you're on the go exploring or soaking up the sights at your hotel, a small backpack is an excellent choice for carrying a few essentials. These backpacks have plenty of room for your travel documents, your camera, and your wallet.

If you're going to be traveling in the warmer weather, a lightweight sundress or bathing suit is another must-have item. During the spring and summer, you'll find that it can get quite warm in Rome, so it's important to pack an outfit with plenty of layers so you can stay cool when the temperature rises.

As well as clothing, you'll also want to carry a few accessories that will help to elevate your outfits and fit in with the style of your destination. Scarves are a popular accessory for both men and women in Rome, so it's worth considering adding a few to your packing list.

Hats are another fashionable option that will keep your head and face warm during the cooler spring and summer evenings. These hats can be worn over a light scarf to give your outfit a touch of sophistication and help you look put together as you explore the city.

To keep your body hydrated, bring a bottle of water with you wherever you go. Rome has a number of fountains and nasoni - public drinking water taps - so make sure you have a reusable water bottle to refill at your convenience.

You can easily buy bottled water in the city, but it's better to save money and plastic waste by investing in a reusable water bottle like this one. It has a built-in LifeStraw water filter so you know that the water is fresh and safe to drink.

You'll also want to consider packing a lightweight pashmina shawl for when you're visiting religious buildings in the city, especially the Vatican, which has a strict dress code that doesn't allow shorts or bare shoulders. A light shawl will keep your neck and shoulders covered during a hot day in Rome and can be folded away into your day bag when you need to head out for the day.

Umbrella

There is no shortage of places to see and things to do in Rome. However, it's also a city that is not immune to bad weather. It can rain more than just the typical drizzle you might expect in other parts of Europe, and even in the summer months, it's possible to experience heavy rainstorms that go on for hours.

Umbrellas are a must for anyone who's visiting the city during the rainy season or any time of year, as they're an essential piece of gear that will make your trip that much easier. They're also a good way to save space in your luggage, as they don't add too much weight to your suitcase.

Aside from being an essential for walking in the rain, an umbrella can also be used to protect you from the sun. They're often worn by people who spend a lot of time outdoors and are designed to protect you from UV rays as well as air humidity.

Another useful item to carry is a pair of sunglasses, as these will help you avoid the sun's harmful UV rays and prevent sunburn. If you're planning on spending a lot of time in the sun, consider investing in some quality sunglasses that will last and are comfortable to wear.

If you're travelling to Rome in the fall, it's a good idea to bring a lightweight jacket or rain hat to keep you warm. These items are easy to pack and can be carried in your day bag ready to use should it start to rain.

You'll probably want to dress smartly for your visit to Rome, so you might also want to bring a light long-sleeved shirt to wear when visiting churches or basilicas that require women to cover their shoulders and knees. A light scarf or shawl can be handy, too.

Tourist Mistakes to Avoid When Traveling To Rome

First, it is imperative to note that you do not need to purchase bottled water in the first place.

The city of Rome has more than 2500 fountains that provide fresh water for its residents. From all around the city of Rome, these fountains dispense crisp, cool water brought to them by the Apennine Mountains or Lake Bracciano. During the summer, bring a bottle to refill from these fountains on a hot day so that you can keep cool. It is still possible to refresh yourself even without a water bottle if you are not carrying one with you. These fountains often have hand pumps so you can refill your cup or hands with fresh water. This is a great way to appreciate the city of Rome and the beautiful fountains that it has to offer. Furthermore, taking a break at a fountain can be a memorable and unique experience, allowing you to experience the artistry and history of the city. Moreover, the fountains in Rome have been around for centuries, so the water from them is not only fresh and clean, but also has an exceptional and refreshing taste. This makes it an even more enjoyable experience for those who take the time to appreciate these beautiful landmarks.

Secondly, we need to remember that not everyone speaks English as a first language.

As one of the least developed countries in Europe in terms of speaking English, Italy remains to be one of the least developed. Despite the fact that Italian has improved a lot over the last few years, especially in metropolises around major tourist attractions, it is recommended that you learn a few basic Italian phrases in addition to "ciao" "grazie" "si" and "no": "Buona giornata", "Buona sera", Il conto per favore", "Dov'e il bagno" means where is the bathroom - will help you interact more effectively with the locals. Knowing a few basic Italian phrases will help you feel more confident when interacting with locals and give you an opportunity to practice speaking Italian. It also shows respect for the culture and will make you more likely to receive positive responses from the locals. An added bonus is that learning Italian phrases may even open the door to meaningful friendships.

It is generally true that Italians are very friendly. If you don't speak their language well, they will still try to communicate with you. If you were able to use just a couple of phrases to explain what you mean, they would appreciate it very much. With a few famous gestures in your hands, along with a few words from the Italian language, you will be ready in no time. Italians are known for their hospitality and warmth, so they are more likely to welcome a stranger regardless of whether they don't understand each other's language. They also appreciate it when people try to make an effort to communicate in Italian, even if they don't fully understand it. Therefore, learning a few phrases is an excellent way to get started in conversation. Even if one is a beginner at Italian, a few well-chosen words and gestures can travel a long way and create a connection with the Italian speaker.

Third, Rome is one of the world's top tourist destinations.

Every year more than 9 million foreign tourists visit the country. This makes it one of the most visited cities in the world. In this city, there are a lot of tourists, which makes the city a hub for robbers and petty thieves who are looking for easy money. In this area, there are a lot of robbers and thieves, which is a result of the abundance of robbers and thieves. These robbers and thieves often take advantage of tourists' unfamiliarity with the area and lack of awareness of local laws and customs. They also often target tourists, as they are more likely to be carrying large amounts of cash. This is because they have expensive electronics, and are more likely to be unfamiliar with the area. As a result, it is imperative for tourists to keep their wits about them and take extra precautions when traveling in this area. This includes avoiding unfamiliar areas, being aware of their surroundings, and not carrying large amounts of cash or valuable items.

In particular, when you're in the metro or crowded places, you need to be aware of your surroundings. Ensure that your valuables and your bags are always under your watch. It is quite common for people to try to give away free stuff to you as one of the most common scams you will come across. Scams like these are often perpetrated by people who are seeking to take advantage of unsuspecting tourists. They may try to get you to purchase something they don't actually have or give you something that is worth much less than what they claim. It is imperative to be on the lookout for these types of scams and to protect your valuables and belongings at all times. To further protect yourself, always be aware of your surroundings and trust your instincts – if something seems too unbelievable to be true, it probably is.

Oftentimes, they will try to convince you that you are getting something for nothing by putting a bracelet on your wrist. The only thing that you need to keep in mind is that once it is on your wrist, you will need to pay them. In the world today, there are an enormous amount of people who are willing to shove roses into your hands. This is until you really have no choice but to hold them. It is true that there are some really helpful people in the local communities who are very keen on helping you out. However, you cannot expect everyone to be helpful or to give you free stuff if you are traveling. This is because those people have their own expenses to take care of and cannot rely on charity. In addition, if you are traveling, you may be in unfamiliar surroundings and not have access to the same resources you have at home. As such, it is imperative to plan ahead and make sure you have enough money to cover all your expenses.

Mistakes made by tourists in Rome

It is true that Rome has so many places to see. You will need at least two, three, or even a week to cover everything that needs to be seen in the city. It is our recommendation that you do not try to cram everything into your itinerary. In addition, you should not even try to take a tour of all the major sites during your stay. Consider your preferences instead, and make a decision about where you really want to spend your time, and then be comfortable with seeing other things from a distance. Perhaps you would rather choose to save some of the items for a future trip to Rome altogether instead of bringing them now. Cramming too much into your itinerary can be overwhelming and cause you to miss out on the beauty and charm of the city. It's imperative to take the time to really experience the unique culture and atmosphere that Rome has to offer. This will enable you to immerse yourself in the sights and sounds that make it so special. By taking the time to savor the unique atmosphere and culture of Rome, you can ensure that you truly soak up the character of the city. You can appreciate it for all that it has to offer. For instance, enjoy a leisurely stroll around the Colosseum and soak in the atmosphere. You can also spend an evening sitting in a cafe people watching and enjoying the sounds of the city. It's like taking the time to savor a fine wine; you can smell the bouquet and appreciate the nuanced flavors that the wine has to offer. It's an experience that you will never forget.

There is nothing better than riding roller coasters at an amusement park as it is one of the most enjoyable things about them.

However, waiting in long lines for rides is one of the most frustrating aspects of amusement parks, because there are so many people! As a matter of fact, the same thing can be said about Rome as well. During the afternoons, there is nothing more frustrating than waiting in this crowded tourist line in the heat of the sun all afternoon in the blazing sun. This is especially true when the attraction in question is small, and there are more people wanting to experience it than the attraction can accommodate. In Rome, the long lines are even more exasperating because the summer heat and humidity can make the wait even more unbearable. When these long lines are encountered in Rome, the summer heat and humidity can make even the most patient person grow increasingly frustrated with the wait.

Therefore, it would be wise to book your entry times or tickets as far in advance as possible to avoid this mistake. The Colosseum, Roman Forum, and Vatican City are some of the most famous monuments in the country as a whole. Make sure you grab a copy of this book to assist you if you are planning on visiting any of the places that you are interested in seeing. Not only will this save you time, but it will also preserve your energy so that you can see as much as possible in Rome. Rome is home to a multitude of incredible sights. With this book, you can easily learn about each monument's history and significance, so you can gain a better understanding and appreciation of the sites.

Additionally, the book offers detailed maps and directions that can help you navigate your way to and from each location quickly. This will ensure that you make the most of your time in Rome.

Let's imagine a hot and sunny day, and there are hundreds, if not thousands, of sweaty tourists pounding the pavement. The list continues on and on, and it encompasses pretty much every single site in Rome during the peak season, every single day of the year. During peak season, the sites tend to be more crowded, making it difficult to view them all on the same day. By rising early or staying out late, you can avoid the crowds and have more time to explore.

You can either take this as an opportunity to take a memorable picture of the setting or just sit on the bench and take it all in. There are plenty of Italians who aren't morning people, and there are plenty of tourists who aren't either. Early in the morning, before 8 a.m., there are fewer people and the weather is cooler, so early mornings are better. You might also want to think about visiting places like the Colosseum after the day is over, as it will be less crowded. Rome is so charming when it is all lit up at night, not only because there are fewer people around, but because there are fewer tourists. This allows visitors to experience the city in a more intimate and peaceful setting. Additionally, the locals tend to be more welcoming when there are fewer tourists around, so visitors can get to know the culture and people better.

Not covering up in churches. In the summer, the weather in Rome can be quite hot, especially if you are visiting during the day.

Tourists can often be seen wearing only minimal clothing when they are on vacation. There is no doubt that it is true that you can go into a church in the middle of the afternoon when you want to cool off. But when you enter churches, you should probably be thinking modesty is in. There are times when people are either turned away at the door or forced to wear these awful papery plastic covers when they need to get to the bathroom. This is because many religious sites require visitors to dress modestly and cover their shoulders and knees. This is seen as a sign of respect and a reflection of the cultural and religious values of the place. Failing to follow this rule could be seen as a sign of disrespect and could even lead to legal repercussions.

As a result, here are a few tips that can help you avoid making the same mistake. If you are planning to wear a hat, remove it, cover your shoulders, cleavage, midriff, and anything visible above your knees. Usually, when we are venturing out, my fiance keeps a sweater, scarf, or even a rain jacket in her backpack. It is not always the case that they check on you, but you should be respectful nonetheless if they do not. This is significant because many places of worship have a dress code that must be followed. By following the tips given, you are showing respect for the place of worship and the people visiting it.

Make sure to stay in the historical center of the city.

The majority of Rome's main sights are located within a relatively small area of central Rome. However, if you don't leave the center at any point, you might miss out on some of the coolest things. There are a few different neighborhoods just a few metro stops away. These neighborhoods will provide you with the opportunity to experience the authentic Rome that locals experience every day in the course of their daily lives. Exploring these different neighborhoods can give you a deeper appreciation of the culture and history of Rome, as well as an insight into the real day-to-day life of the city. Plus, you'll be able to discover hidden gems and restaurants off the beaten path that you would never have known existed if you stayed in the center.

There are a lot of things to do in Trastevere in particular. There is no longer a secret about this neighborhood, and nowadays you will see hordes of tourists enjoying this neighborhood. As a general rule, any walk along the Tiber River will lead you to some local-only bars and restaurants, but for the most part, you'll be walking among the locals. In addition, if you are near the Vatican, you might want to consider checking out the town of Prati. Prati is a much quieter and more residential area, but it still has plenty of things to do for visitors. It's full of hidden gems, from local restaurants serving traditional Italian dishes to charming shops and cafes to explore. Plus, it's just a short walk from the Vatican, making it easy and convenient to explore the sights in both neighborhoods.

There are some of the most prestigious restaurants in the city operating here, and this is one of the more affluent parts of the city. In the southeast part of the city, there is a neighborhood called Testaccio that is an excellent example of this. This is one of the most desirable neighborhoods to find authentic Roman food in the city. It is also the most local area out of the three neighborhoods we have mentioned, as well as the most authentic. Testaccio has a lot of character and charm, with some of the most well-known restaurants in the city. It is also home to some of the highest quality Roman food in the city, with its traditional eateries, trattorias, and pizzerias. It is an excellent place to experience local culture and sample some of the region's most delicious cuisine.

Chapter 9.
Rome Fun facts

Here are some fun facts and trivia about Rome:

Rome is known as the "Eternal City" because it was believed that no matter what happened to the world, Rome would always remain standing.

Rome is the capital city of Italy and also the largest city in the country.

The Colosseum is one of the most iconic landmarks in Rome. It was built in 80 AD and is considered one of the greatest examples of Roman architecture.

The Vatican City is an independent state located within Rome. It is the smallest country in the world and the headquarters of the Roman Catholic Church.

Rome has a rich culinary history, with traditional dishes like spaghetti carbonara, cacio e pepe, and saltimbocca alla romana.

The Pantheon is a famous ancient Roman temple that was later converted into a church. It is the best-preserved ancient Roman building in the city.

Rome has a total of 280 fountains, with the most famous being the Trevi Fountain. Legend says that if you throw a coin over your shoulder into the fountain, you will one day return to Rome.

The Spanish Steps is a popular tourist attraction in Rome, with 138 steps leading up to the Trinità dei Monti church.

Rome is home to many famous museums, including the Vatican Museums, the Capitoline Museums, and the Galleria Borghese.

The phrase "All roads lead to Rome" refers to the fact that Rome was the hub of the ancient Roman road network, with roads leading from all parts of the Roman Empire to the city.

Rome has a rich history, with ruins dating back to ancient Rome, including the Roman Forum and the Circus Maximus.

The Italian language is derived from Latin, which was the language spoken in ancient Rome.

Rome is located on the banks of the Tiber River, which is the third-longest river in Italy.

Rome is home to the largest Baroque fountain in the world, the Fontana di Trevi.

The city of Rome has been inhabited for over 2,500 years, making it one of the oldest continuously inhabited cities in the world.

Rome was the birthplace of many famous historical figures, including Julius Caesar, Augustus, and Constantine the Great.

Rome has a Mediterranean climate, with hot summers and mild winters.

The city is home to two major football clubs, A.S. Roma and S.S. Lazio, both of which have a strong following.

Rome is a popular filming location, with many movies and TV shows shot in the city, including "Roman Holiday" and "The Great Beauty."

Conclusion

Rome is a destination for anyone who wants to learn about its history and culture, enjoy an outdoor vacation with family, or indulge in a culinary journey. Because there are so many attractions in Rome and so much to do there, visitors can choose how they want to explore it by deciding what trip they need. From just walking around the major monuments and sites to spending days touring Italy, from food tours to museums, there is no better time than now for you to go!

Rome is one of the most visited cities in Europe. Rome has been the capital of Italy continuously since 1870 and has a population of over 2.7 million residents. The largest urban area in the region of Lazio is Rome, with a population of 3.7 million.

Having the best guide enables one to visit the best places to see, the best restaurants to taste, and the best shops for shopping. The local guide is your most knowledgeable local guide with a good knowledge of the history of Rome and a comprehensive understanding of many other little-known facts.

The city has everything from fine dining to quick eats such as paninis and pizza. Italian favorites are available, along with some traditional Roman dishes. Some restaurants even have rooftops that allow diners to enjoy beautiful city views while enjoying their meal. Pizza is a popular dish because it is delicious, quick, and fun to make, but there are also numerous other options for those who want something else when dining out in Rome.

Below is a map of Rome that will help you on your journey.

Have a great vacation!

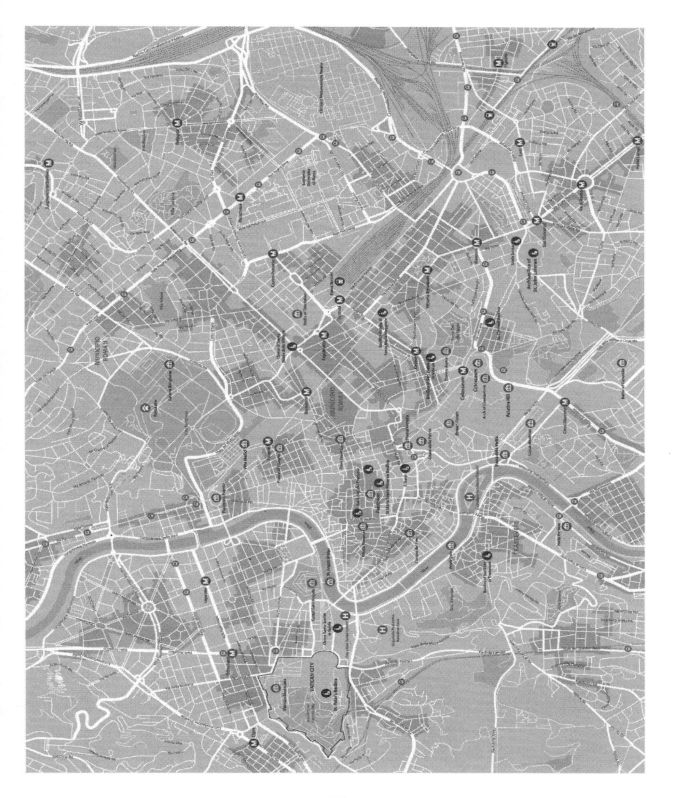